BOURNEMOUTH INTERNATIONAL AIRPORT

BOURNEMOUTH INTERNATIONAL AIRPORT

Mike Phipp

TEMPUS

The opening of the Bournemouth Aviation Museum in May 1998 was marked with demonstration flights by a number of their historic jet fighters, also coinciding with a visit from Concorde to the airport whilst operating a charter to Paris.

First published 2002
Copyright © Mike Phipp, 2002

Tempus Publishing Limited
The Mill, Brimscombe Port,
Stroud, Gloucestershire, GL5 2QG
www.tempus-publishing.com

ISBN 0 7524 2396 7

TYPESETTING AND ORIGINATION BY
Tempus Publishing Limited
PRINTED IN GREAT BRITAIN BY
Midway Colour Print, Wiltshire

Contents

Acknowledgements   7

Introduction   8

1.   Wartime Operations   9

2.   Airline Operations   21

3.   Military Activity   61

4.   Vickers-Armstrongs & BAC   76

5.   FR Aviation   85

6.   Additional Businesses & Operations   93

7.   Present-Day Operations   111

A sunny welcome greets prospective passengers at the entrance of the airport's present-day terminal building.

Acknowledgements

My thanks go especially to two earlier contributors to the Tempus Publishing range – Barry Abraham and Colin Cruddas – for their encouragement for me to 'go it alone' with this publication after helping them with their earlier research.

The main source of information and photographs has been the Archive Room at the airport which the author has been building up over the years. As is often the case, many of the photographs are uncredited, and, despite research, the author apologizes to those who have been overlooked. My thanks to the following who have provided additional information and photographs to fill the gaps: Warren Brown, Tony Dean, Eric Hayward, Betty Hockey, Ron McConkie, Tony Needham, Ron Palin, John Peatty, Ray Sturtivant, Noel White and members of 397 Bomb Group Association

Also acknowledgement and thanks to the following for delving into their archives: BAe, Bournemouth Aviation Museum, Bournemouth Daily Echo, CSE Citation Centre, European Aviation, FR Aviation, Key Publishing, VT Aerospace.

As is the custom, special thanks to my wife, who, as well as having to proof-read, has frequently found that I have disappeared, yet again, down to the airport – all in the cause of research!

Introduction

This book has resulted from the photographic display held in the airport terminal during the summer of 2001 to mark the 60th anniversary of the opening of RAF Hurn. Having put together a large collection of photographs, it seemed natural to spend a little more time in gathering together others for publication in book form. The airport was briefly covered in the Images of Aviation volume entitled *In Dorset's Skies*, with this new title continuing on the theme and expanding the historical detail. However, nothing startling in the way of new information has been discovered, and whilst a few aircraft covered are duplicated, they are mainly with replacement photographs.

Bournemouth had an early association with international aviation, with continental flyers appearing at the Centenary Aviation Meeting in July 1910, followed by the town hosting the Schneider Races in September 1919. During the First World War pilot training was undertaken at Ensbury Park, also known as RFC Winton, to the north of the town. With the return to peace there were attempts to establish air services, but these did not prove popular, so the site became a racecourse in 1925. A number of air races were also held, but the racecourse company went out of business in 1928 and the site was developed for housing. (There's nothing new in this world!).

Bournemouth did not proceed with initial thoughts for a Municipal Aerodrome in 1930, despite the recommendations of Sir Alan Cobham, who went on to become a director of Bournemouth Airport Ltd at neighbouring Christchurch. Later attempts by Bournemouth and Poole to build a Joint Municipal Aerodrome at Moor Town again came to nothing. Although the land was purchased, expenditure on further development was beyond the means of the councils. (This was repeated in 1994 when further funding was required to expand Bournemouth International Airport). Sir Alan Cobham again considered land at East Parley in 1938 as the site of an aerodrome, but the Lord of the Manor was totally opposed to such an idea. So Bournemouth still did not have its own airport.

Wartime needs saw the construction of an airfield which had a military life of only three years before becoming, briefly, the UK's major civil airport. Since then the airport has seen many ups and downs, with a variety of activities over the years. This has been one of the attractions for aviation enthusiasts – one never knows what type of aircraft might turn up. The author recalls the BOAC crew training days of the early fifties, when a ditch alongside the perimeter road proved useful if the approaching Comet appeared too low! Never a major airport, Bournemouth serves the local holiday travellers, and a comment given by Alan Whicker in an interview in 2001 sums it up. 'It reminds me of once-upon-a-time Northolt. The amenities are uncrowded, the queues small and unpushy. There's no doubt airports are pleasanter places when they're almost empty'. I am sure the majority of passengers agree.

One

Wartime Operations

The siting of Bournemouth International Airport can be traced back to 1929 when Bournemouth Council requested Sir Alan Cobham to find a suitable site for an aerodrome. The Air Ministry had contacted the council the previous autumn advising that they 'should consider earnestly the advisability of establishing a Municipal Aerodrome'. Sir Alan delivered his report in April 1930, listing various options, including land north of the town at East Parley which was 'capable of being made into a magnificent aerodrome'. However the council decided not to proceed with any development at the time, and Sir Alan became involved in other aviation projects.

On the outbreak of the Second World War the majority of Britain's military airfields were on the eastern side of the country – closest to Germany. The situation was turned on its head with the invasion of the Low Countries and France, the prospect of the invasion of Britain during Operation Sealion and the Battle of Britain in the summer of 1940. These events showed that air defence was needed for military installations in the south, and that airfields would have to be provided quickly as it was feared that Operation Sealion had only been postponed until the following year. The Air Ministry were aware of the land available at East Parley, which they requisitioned in 1940 for the construction of a fighter base. Built to the then standard airfield pattern, there were three intersecting runways, 'frying-pan' dispersals on the northern side, with living quarters in the woods around the nearby Hurn village.

RAF Station Hurn opened on 1 August 1941 nominally as a fighter station under No.11 Group, but no aircraft were based there at the time. The Germans did not proceed with Operation Sealion during 1941 and so some of the pressure for fighter cover was removed. The first arrival was a Whirlwind fighter, which crash landed on 6 August having suffered an engine failure returning from operations, striking builders equipment on the runway and suffering the indignity of ending up on its nose. The first occupants during the autumn of 1941 were the trials aircraft of the Telecommunication Flying Unit's Research Section, which were involved in the development of airborne radar. An airborne interception system had already been developed for operational use in Beaufighter night fighters. This was followed by a development for bombers, which became known as H2S in operational service, being initially tested in a Blenheim, followed by a Halifax. The Unit operated in conjunction with the Telecommunications Research Establishment's site at Worth Matravers in the Purbecks and the recently opened radar station at Sopley. However the fear of a surprise attack by the Germans to capture the radar secrets from the various sites led to the Unit being moved inland at the end of May 1942 to Defford which was considered a safer location.

June 1942 saw Hurn transferred to No.38 Wing, Army Co-Operation Command, and the arrival of Whitley Vs which were used for paratroop training. Horsa gliders began to appear in September, frequently being towed by the Whitleys to Salisbury Plain to take part in Army exercises. The RAF moved out in the autumn to make way for the USAAF, which used the airfield as a major base for troops departing for Operation Torch; the Allied invasion of North Africa. Six B-17F Fortresses flew VIPs to Gibraltar on 5 November – including General Eisenhower and Major General Jimmy Doolittle, with one of the pilots being Paul Tibbets who later found 'fame' as the B-29 pilot who dropped the atom bomb at Hiroshima. The B-17s were followed by large numbers of C-47 Skytrains, plus further B-17s and B-24 Liberators as transports.

The Air Ministry decided that Hurn would be a suitable additional base for BOAC, who were operating flying boat services from nearby Poole Harbour. In January 1942 irregular services commenced to Egypt and other Mediterranean destinations operated by Curtiss CW-20 St Louis and two Liberator transports. The Cairo service did not get off to a good start as one of the Liberators was shot down in error over the Channel whilst returning home. Although BOAC had come into being in April 1940, the majority of their wartime aircraft carried small 'British Airways' titles. Dakotas began to appear in the spring of 1943, plus further Liberator transports, and the airline was responsible for the 'VIP hangar' at Hurn which, amongst others, housed Winston Churchill's Liberator transport Commando during 1942/43.

No.38 Wing returned at the beginning of 1943 to re-equip with Albemarles, and large number of Horsas arrived in preparation for Operation Beggar – the Allied invasion of Sicily from North Africa. They were towed out by Halifaxes on 1 June, stopping off at Portreath to refuel prior to the long flight to Gibraltar and then on to Oran in Algeria. Nothing like this had been attempted before, and as a trial to test the endurance of aircraft and crew, a Halifax/Horsa flew around the country from nearby Holmsley South, landing at Hurn ten hours and 1,400 miles later. The Albemarles flew out separately to Oran in order to tow some of the Horsas across the Mediterranean, being the first operational use of the type. Additional Albemarles seen in June were those of the Russian Army Air Force, the crews of which being trained by the local squadrons. The Red Starred bombers making the locals look twice in amazement! With No.38 Wing's need to expand its glider training duties there were frequent exercises, during which many of the Horsas ended up scattered around the area, with one enterprising Throop schoolboy charging his pals 3d to see over the glider before it was reclaimed by the RAF. During the winter of 1943/44 expansion of the airfield was carried out, with many new hardstandings being added to the north west.

March 1944 saw the departure of the Albemarles and Horsas with the transfer of Hurn to 11 Group, Fighter Command, in preparation for a new role. During the previous autumn the RAF had assigned many of its fighter squadrons to the newly formed 2nd Tactical Air Force in preparation for the forthcoming invasion of Europe, and many were to pass through Hurn during the summer of 1944. Three squadrons of Canadian aircrew arrived in March 1944 with newly acquired Typhoon fighter bombers, to form No.143 (RCAF) Fighter Wing. Their Typhoons carried two underwing 1,000lb bombs, the Wing becoming operational at the end of April with attacks on V-1 sites. April also saw the arrival of three further Typhoon squadrons to form No.124 Fighter Wing, these being equipped with underwing rockets. The Typhoons were joined by two Mosquito night fighter squadrons to provide cover for the invasion forces, the fighters concentrating their attacks on enemy radar sites in order to put them out of action prior to the invasion. However, operations over Northern France were not without hazards, as even the high ranking officers found out. No.143's Wing Commander crash landed in Normandy in May following an engine failure, and spent his time evading capture, 124's Wing Commander's Typhoon was hit over Dieppe later in the month, ditching in the Channel and being rescued by an ASR Walrus, and one of the Squadron Leader's suffered a similar fate. In preparation for their anticipated move to Normandy, the Squadrons practised landing on short, temporary airstrips with an 800 yard section marked out alongside the runway, the pilots soon became proficient at using it. Another unit formed at Hurn was to train racing pigeons to bring back messages from Normandy in the first few days after the invasion – flight time seven hours! So on the eve of D-Day, Hurn hosted two Mosquito night fighter squadrons and six Typhoon fighter bomber squadrons. One final task awaited the fighters – this was for ground crews to paint the black and white 'Invasion Stripes' around the wings and rear fuselage as a recognition feature.

D-Day 6 June 1944 and Operation Overlord saw allied forces cross the English Channel by air and sea, with massive aerial activity all along the South Coast. At Hurn the three RCAF Typhoon squadrons were despatched at 7.25 a.m. to bomb gun emplacements in Normandy just as the first landing craft were making shore, and during the day the Typhoons attacked various enemy positions, including gun emplacements, tanks and troops – a total of eighty-eight sorties by the six squadrons. The long hours of daylight meant that on subsequent days the fighters could begin operations at about 3.00 a.m. and continue until 11.30 p.m. at night, leaving the ground crews only a few hours to service the aircraft. 7 June saw one hundred and thirty-eight sorties, with one hundred and thirty-four on 8 June. With the success of Operation Overlord, the allies were soon able to construct Advance Landing Grounds in Normandy, which enabled the fighters to land to re-arm and re-fuel. However these strips threw up a lot of dust which adversely effected the Typhoon's engines, resulting in the squadrons returning to Hurn each evening for servicing or replacement engines. Another problem was that many of the strips were still within range of the German guns! June and July saw the coming and going of many Typhoon squadrons – out of a total of twenty operational squadrons at the time, fifteen passed through Hurn. Some did not carry out operations, they just found the hard runway at Hurn more suitable for departure to Normandy than the grass strips they had been using.

Following the departure of the Typhoons, the Mosquito squadrons remained, to be joined on 29 June by six USAAF P-61 Black Widow night fighters. These had newly arrived in Britain, but the USAAF were not certain whether they would prove such an effective night fighter as the Mosquito, so it was arranged that they would gain experience alongside the RAF in order to prove their value. In the end the P-61s showed themselves to be faster than, and able to out-turn, the Mosquitoes, which shocked the RAF top brass as well as some of those of the USAAF. The P-61s returned to their home base on 10 July, prior to beginning operations from Normandy later in the month, and by the end of the month both Mosquito Squadrons had also moved out.

The reason for the move was that Hurn was transferred to USAAF control at the beginning of August, becoming Station 492 for the arrival of four squadrons of B-26B Marauders. These formed the 397th Bomb Group, and many were silver coloured, often with bright nose markings – a contrast to the drab camouflage of the RAF Mosquitoes and Typhoons. The Group's stay was short, with the last of the squadrons crossing to Normandy on the 31 August. During their stay the Group undertook its 100th wartime mission on 16 August, which was an attack on railway installations near Paris. On their return home, the pilots celebrated the event by firing very flares out of the cockpit windows, setting fire to the local farmer's field – they were not amused! In spite of their short stay at Hurn, the Group seem to be remembered most out of all the wartime operators, with their veterans keeping in close contact and making a final farewell visit to their wartime base in the summer of 2000. Although the B-26s had moved across the Channel, the airfield remained under USAAF control until mid-October, by which time RAF Hurn's wartime activities were at an end.

A June 1942 view of RAF Hurn showing major extensions underway to the north of the airfield to accommodate the many fighters that would be based there during D-Day. Also evident are the 'hedge' camouflaging across the existing airfield and the lack of hangars.

Opposite below: Armstrong Whitworth Albemarles were the unwanted bombers of the war, and eventually it was decided to use them within 38 Wing for special forces duties and towing Horsa gliders. Three squadrons were based at Hurn during 1943/44, the type undertaking its first operational mission in July 1943. 297 Squadron was one of the Hurn-based squadrons which operated the Albemarle, with the glider towing equipment clearly visible in this post D-Day view.

Wartime conditions inside the Control Tower, or Watch Tower as it was known at the time, as flying operations were only watched, not controlled. This August 1944 view shows operations being conducted by the USAAF who were based on the airfield at the time.

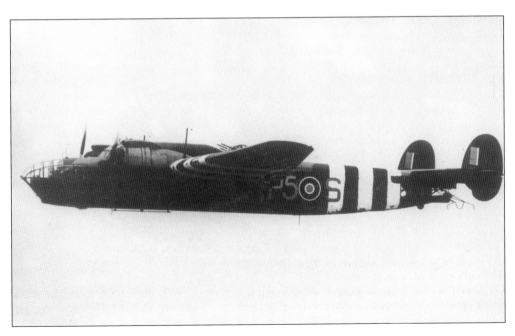

From the summer of 1942 until the spring of 1944, large numbers of Airspeed Horsa troop-carrying gliders were to be seen at Hurn undertaking training exercises in preparation for the invasion of Europe. Here troops are seen preparing to embark on one such exercise.

Three Canadian Typhoon squadrons formed No.143 Wing, and their Leader, Wing Commander R. Davidson, is seen just prior to D-Day with his 'personal' Typhoon carrying his initials RD as code. Ground transport is a Bournemouth-registered Norton motorcycle.

Bombed up and ready to go, Flight Officer Reilly and Pilot Officer Duncan of 440 (RCAF) Squadron pose by a suitably inscribed 1,000lb bomb – 'May we drop one for you?' 143 Wing's Typhoons carrying one such bomb under each wing.

A Mosquito XIII night fighter of 604 Squadron sets off on a training mission during June 1944, and below it can be seen Typhoons parked along the southern perimeter of the airfield. Along with 125 Squadron, Mosquitoes of 604 helped provide cover for the invasion forces.

Aircrew from 'A' Flight of 604 Squadron appear happy as they pose in front of one of their Mosquito XIIIs. Note the enlarged nose containing the AI radar scanner. The squadron undertook a hectic three months of operations whilst based at Hurn.

As with all wartime airfields, large numbers of 'temporary' maycrete buildings were erected for a variety of uses. On the airfield's north-west side, this one served as part of the wartime laboratory block, and is still in use at the present time – sixty years on.

A number of hangars on the north-west side of the airfield were for use by BOAC, who required further accommodation when they expanded their operations at the end of 1944. This is one of two similar hangars built for them at the end of the war – here seen in the 1990s.

597th BOMB SQDN.

598th BOMB SQDN.

596th BOMB SQDN.

599th BOMB SQDN.

397th BOMB GROUP ASSOCIATION

Although only being based on the airfield for a few weeks in August 1944, the B-26 Marauder crews of the USAAF 397th Bomb Group remember their stay at Hurn with affection. This postcard shows the badges of the Group's four Bomb Squadrons.

Some of the American crew from the 397th Bomb Group who were based at Hurn during 1944, and were part of the USAAF's 9th Air Force. The B-26 carries the usual nose art and still carries drab camouflage, the majority at Hurn being in natural metal finish.

The USAAF were also represented at Hurn by a few P-61 Black Widow night fighters during July 1944. Seen on the north-east side of the airfield, aircraft of 422 & 425 Night Fighter Squadron undertook competitive trials with Mosquito night fighters of 125 Squadron.

The 397th Bomb Group moved from Rivenhall to Hurn to be closer to their targets. Crews from the Group display one of the 1,000lb bombs they carried in their B-26 Maruaders. *Innocents Abroad* carries over sixty bombing mission symbols under its cockpit.

In June 2000 the Airport was honoured to host a nostalgic return visit from the United States by some of the 397th Bomb Group's wartime crews. The jeep added to the atmosphere, with memories stirred by a flight in a Dakota (or should that be C-47?).

Douglas C-47s / Dakotas have always been part of the scene at Hurn – whether of RAF, USAAF or BOAC. No squadrons or units were permanently based at the airfield – the largest number at any time being from the USAAF who were passing through during November 1942.

Two

Airline Operations

Well before the end of the War the Air Ministry were considering Hurn's future use. During the spring of 1944 the RAF undertook a review of Hurn for its probable use by Transport Command, but in August were advised by the Air Ministry that the airfield was to be allotted to BOAC as a temporary measure until Heath Row was available. BOAC's existing base at Whitchurch was unsatisfactory for their expanding operations, and Hurn was considered suitable as it was close to their flying boat bases at Hythe and Poole. However BOAC did express concern at the lack of suitable hangars in view of the anticipated increase in its long range fleet to forty or fifty aircraft. In October BOAC confirmed that its passenger and freight services would transfer from Whitchurch, but Liberator and York maintenance would be undertaken at RAF Lyneham as Hurn's hangars were not suitable.

The airport was transferred from RAF Fighter Command to the Director General of Civil Aviation as from 23.00 hours on 31 October 1944 for development as the UK's civil air terminal. BOAC had already been operating limited services from Hurn and had also set up a Development Flight in January 1944 for testing new British airliners and engines prior to their entering service. The move from Whitchurch led to the expansion of services, with Dakotas operating to Cairo, Lisbon and Madrid as from 1 November. Existing services were improved to Karachi and West Africa, plus Yorks added on the flights to Cairo. As well as BOAC, there were some services by KLM to Lisbon with Dakotas, ABA Swedish Airlines from Stockholm, also with Dakotas, and Sabena from Leopoldville with a Lodestar, the airlines having to use terminal facilities situated in the former RAF buildings at Hurn Village, some way from the airport. Passenger comfort in the aircraft was not a high priority, with most of the Dakotas retaining their military style seating.

Early in 1945 BOAC finalized plans for a major new service to Sydney operated by Lancastrians, with accommodation limited to nine 'day' passengers or six 'night' ones, plus Royal Mail. Crew training was undertaken, and a proving flight departed on 23 April, being extended to Auckland – a total of 13,500 miles. For political reasons BOAC did not want the service publicised, in fact some of the Lancastrians appeared in RAF colours, but by the time services commenced on 31 May the aircraft had reappeared in BOAC colours. Wartime needs meant that travel was only available to those in the services or sponsored by a government department, and the route 'served the needs of the Far Eastern theatre of war'. Operated in conjunction with Qantas, the new 'Kangaroo' service was also known as 'Three Dawns to Sydney', reflecting the three night stops taken.

Towards the end of 1944 consideration was given to a major expansion of the airport, although extension of the main 6,000ft runway would 'entail diversion of the fairly important Hurn-Wimborne road'. The new Ministry of Civil Aviation planned a £1.25 million development as the terminal for services to South Africa and South America. A change of Government in July 1945 saw the plans scrapped and the intended Transport Command base to the west of London, known as RAF Heath Row, was developed. At the time BOAC were operating seventy-four services a week, and in November the Ministry confirmed 'Hurn will be a major terminal until suitable airports nearer London are available'.

At the end of the War, both Pan American World and American Airlines were operating flying boat services across the Atlantic to Shannon, where they connected with a BOAC Dakota to Croydon. Both airlines planned landplane services from New York to London, but it would be some while before the new London Airport, as Heath Row was renamed, was available. The Ministry of Civil Aviation offered them facilities at Bournemouth which was not considered convenient by the Americans, but they had to accept it. Both used Douglas DC-4 Skymasters, with Pan American's first proving flight arriving on 18 September 1945, followed by American's a week later. Pan American planned its first service on 20 October, but problems with their DC-4s meant that the first scheduled service was by American Airlines, with *Flagship London* arriving on 24 October. The airline's publicity quoted London as the destination, not pointing out that passengers would arrive at Bournemouth, with their journey being completed by train or coach. Flying time was twenty-four hours, including two refuelling stops, with services from Chicago, Philadelphia and Washington soon following. In conjunction with South African Airways, BOAC commenced services to Johannesburg in November with luxury-appointed Yorks (twelve seat plus mail), initially taking four days to reach Johannesburg. At the beginning of 1946 both American and Pan American began to receive faster Lockheed Constellations, with Pan American's first service arriving on 12 February having taken only twelve hours from New York, and being the first civilian landplane to fly direct from the USA to England.

London Airport was officially opened on 31 May 1946 and the airlines transferred their services, even though there were very limited facilities. No hangars were available and there was only a tented terminal area, but the passengers did arrive in London. With the importance of Bournemouth gone, the Air Ministry described it as a satellite to London, but the airport continued to see airliners of the major airlines. One reason was the lack of maintenance facilities at London which meant that BOAC's fleet of Lancastrians and Yorks had to return for servicing. Known as their No.2 Maintenance Line and employing 1,500 staff, the unit was responsible for aircraft used on the African and Far Eastern services. The airline also continued to use the airport for crew training. Secondly, the new London Airport was frequently affected by fog (or smog as it was known in those days) which resulted in flights being diverted to Bournemouth due to its better weather. Records for the winter of 1946 show that 257 diverted aircraft carried 1,735 passengers with 1,342 crew – 1.3 passengers per crew! BOAC moved its maintenance to London in the spring of 1950, but major diversions continued until the early 1960s when jet airliners took over from the piston ones. BOAC's Development Flight remained to test new airliners such as the Hermes, Dove and Argonaut, being visited by the prototype Comet I jet as early as November 1949.

In May 1947 local travel firm R.E. Bath operated holiday charters to Basle with Doves of International Airways, being the start of Bath's holiday package flights which greatly expanded during the 1960/70s. International were awarded a BEA Associate Agreement in 1948 to operate from Croydon to Cowes and Bournemouth with services flown by Dragon Rapides, but there was little business and the service only lasted a few weeks. Their advert also showed admission to the airport's public enclosure at 3d, with teas and light refreshments being available. Terminal facilities were now established in buildings adjacent to the main apron and June 1952 saw the commencement of regular services to the Channel Islands, being flown by Dragon Rapides of Jersey Airlines. One problem for travellers was the lack of a Customs Office at the airport, with an officer having to come by taxi from Poole Quay to meet each flight. Independent Air Travel set up business in the spring of 1955 operating a Dove, mainly on cross Channel charters, although more ambitious charters to Majorca were proposed. The following spring the airline acquired three Vikings which entered service on charter and IT flights, and in 1957 two DC-4 Skymasters were added. In the autumn of 1958 local travel firm Bath Travel operated two holiday flights to Majorca, using Independent Vikings, and as both flights were soon filled they were repeated the following autumn with BEA Viscounts. The local residents acquired a taste for holiday flights from their local airport, and these Palmair flights have expanded ever since. Air Safaris was another airline based at Bournemouth early in 1960, operating Hermes and Vikings mainly on IT flights out of Gatwick. The airline planned a number of services from Bournemouth to European destinations with its Vikings, the first being to Ostend and Amsterdam in April 1961, followed a few days later by Dublin and Belfast. Other routes were planned, but the airline ran into financial difficulties and went out of business in October with most of the fleet sold for scrap – £360 for a Hermes and £130 for a Viking! This was the pattern of services from Bournemouth for the next thirty years – to the Channel Islands mainly for holidays, northwards to the likes of Manchester and Scotland for business, plus fledgling airlines trying to commence business.

The summer of 1960 saw demonstration flights by the new Dart-Herald and in September Jersey Airlines ordered six, being the first firm order for the aircraft. These entered service on the Jersey route in May 1961 and were to be part of the Bournemouth scene until April 1999 when the type was withdrawn from service. Nearby Southampton Airport had been suffering with waterlogged runways during the winter months for some years, with many services diverted. The airport was sold in the spring of 1961 and its airlines switched to Bournemouth – BEA operating Viscounts to Jersey, Cambrian Dakotas to Paris and Silver City Superfreighters to the Channel Islands and Cherbourg, resulting in a new car ferry terminal being brought into use as Silver City estimated they would be operating thirty-six return services a day, enabling many local people to enjoy the experience of taking their car across the Channel.

The Ministry of Aviation announced plans in July 1960 for a £250,000 terminal, designed to handle sixteen flights and 400 passengers an hour, which would make Bournemouth 'a very important provincial airport'. A new fire station was also included, but while this was being built, the terminal plans were abandoned on financial grounds, and a Government White Paper the following year resulted in the airport being put up for sale. Preliminary talks were held with Bournemouth Council to see if they were interested, the Ministry mistakenly believing it was within their boundary whereas at the time it was within that of Ringwood & Fordingbridge RDC! It was to take eight years of wrangling before the airport was finally purchased by the local authorities. In the autumn of 1962 the Ministry announced that it would withdraw twenty-four hour cover as the airport was no longer required as a diversionary airfield. One reason was that it could not handle the Boeing 707s and Douglas DC-8s now in service, and secondly the Ministry were no longer interested in running Bournemouth.

In January 1962 Silver City became part of the British United Group, being joined by Jersey Airlines in November, and although there were no immediate changes, British United titles appeared on their aircraft the following year. From April 1965 Palmair introduced British United's new One-Elevens on the fortnightly Palma holiday service, now being marketed as Palmair Express. Over at Southampton a concrete runway had been completed by its new owner and from 1 April 1966 the airlines transferred back to Southampton. One reason was the better road and rail connections at Southampton, but the major reason was the Ministry's lack of interest in Bournemouth, where operating hours were reduced to weekdays only as from November – no incentive for airlines or other operators. The summer of 1965 had seen 195,000 passengers use Bournemouth, but there were only 45,000 in the summer of 1966. Many of these were on IT holiday flights, the only scheduled services remaining being two days a week to Jersey by British United and once a week to Paris by Cambrian – both services finishing at the end of October with the introduction of the reduced operating hours. So for the first time in fourteen years, Bournemouth was left without scheduled services – the outlook was bleak.

Negotiations with the Board of Trade (who had taken over the Ministry of Aviation) were protracted, they were hopeful of a sale to a consortium of Bournemouth and Hampshire Councils, but Hampshire pulled out in July 1967. Its place was taken by Dorset, and eventually the airport was sold to Bournemouth and Dorset Councils for £750,000 on 1 April 1969. It must be remembered that at the time the airport was still in Hampshire – it did not 'move' into Dorset until boundary changes in 1974. Operating hours were extended, taking in weekends again, and at the end of 1969 there was a 'change' of name to Bournemouth-Hurn Airport.

Luckily Bournemouth did not have to wait too long for new services. Local travel firm Kentways organized holiday IT flights to Majorca, being operated fortnightly from April 1967 by Douglas DC-7s, being replaced by Coronado jets of Spantax from the following March. More important was the renewal of the Channel Island routes by Channel Airways of Southend, who commenced a weekday service in June 1967 operated by HS.748s and Viscounts – the airport also seeing an increase in Channel Island freight business. Bournemouth saw its first Boeing 707 when one from Canadian airline Wardair was diverted from Gatwick in January 1971. However this was beaten by Freddie Laker and his Skytrain DC-10 which visited in December 1972 during a round the country demonstration flight. During the winter of 1971/72 Channel Airways ran into financial difficulties, suspending its Channel Island services at the end of February. As a stop gap British Midland took over, but the route was awarded to Dan-Air as from 1 July using HS.748s. Dan-Air had already commenced a 'Link-City' service from Bournemouth to Newcastle in April, also with HS.748s, and their Comet 4s were to be seen on IT flights. A recession in the country during the mid-1970s saw a downturn in the IT holiday market, with Kentways going out of business in the winter of 1974 and Palmair reporting a 50% drop in passenger numbers by early 1977. However there was an increase in freight traffic, mainly flowers and produce from the Channel Islands, with the hangar by the terminal becoming the dedicated Cargo Terminal. This was especially busy in August 1972 during Operation Redskin when large amounts of tomatoes had to be flown over from the Channel Islands due to a seaman's strike. Express Air Freight started operating Dakota freighters in the autumn of 1977 on the Channel Islands route, being joined by Dart Heralds in the following January. From February 1980 they commenced the nightly Royal Mail letter service from Bournemouth to Liverpool, soon carrying 50,000 items of mail from the Wessex area. The airline changed its name to Channel Express in the summer of 1982 to reflect its main area of operation, expanding its road distribution network with a fleet of refrigerated lorries to deliver the flowers flown in from the Channel Islands to UK markets. The spring of 1982 saw Dan-Air's 'Link-City' service operated by Metropolitan Airways with Twin Otters, leaving just the Channel Island services to Dan-Air. Metropolitan introduced Short 330s from the spring of 1984, but went into liquidation in August 1985. A number of firms tried to replace the Manchester service which was popular with businessmen, but none were successful.

The spring of 1983 saw the road adjacent to the airfield diverted away from the southern end of the main runway to provide a safe overrun area, and the first half of the new terminal was built at a cost of £1.5m. The terminal was brought into use at a time when there was a reduction in the number of scheduled services, although IT traffic had increased, and in the summer 1986 bids were sought by the councils for the take over of airport operations – the airport becoming a plc in November 1986. This followed a Government directive that airports could no longer be run by local authorities, but in the event the councils continued management under the banner of the plc (both being 50% shareholders) which commenced business on 1 April 1987.

Application was made to the EEC for funding for the second half of the terminal, but the airport was informed that Bournemouth was not in the correct part of England to qualify! Over the years there have been many proposals for Bournemouth to take the overspill from Heathrow and Gatwick, by taking on some of their IT flights. However there were the problems of finding capital to improve the infrastructure, plus objections from residents over the perceived increased noise from additional traffic.

Jersey European applied to operate services to Jersey from the spring of 1987 in competition with Dan-Air, who then withdrew its winter service, saying that it was only economic to operate during the summer months. So Jersey European hastily started services in January, initially with Short 360s and later Friendships. However the decline in Channel Islands passenger traffic resulted in Jersey European reducing its service to just one flight a day in the winter of 1991, but worse was to come when the service ceased completely at the end of the summer 1993 season, just leaving Bournemouth with holiday IT flights. The Palmair flights suffered a number of problems at the beginning of the 1990s, due to a number of airlines going out of business. So for their 1993 season Bath Travel introduced their own aircraft – the Palmair name genuinely taking to the air, services commencing on 1 April with a BAe.146 which soon received the passengers seal of approval. An attempt to re-establish scheduled services saw the launch of Euro Direct in April 1994, with services to European capitals, plus internal flights. Regrettably all services ceased in February 1995 due to the withdrawal of financial backing, plus high landing fees in Europe. Dorset County Council confirmed that it had no funds available to contribute towards the airport's expansion, and Bournemouth were in a similar situation. Both councils, as shareholders, agreed that external financial backing would be required for any future development.

Even before the end of the Second World War, BOAC resumed services to Australia with Avro Lancastrians. G-AGLF was the first of the fleet, with G-AGLV commencing services from Bournemouth to Sydney on 31 May 1945. Avro Tudor IIs were planned as replacements.

BOAC set up their Development Flight at Bournemouth in 1944, initially with Lancaster G-AGJI which was camouflaged in common with the airline's Dakotas and Yorks. After an overhaul in 1945 the Lancaster reappears in shining silver, but still keeping its bomb doors.

BOURNEMOUTH
INTERNATIONAL
AIRPORT

BRITAIN'S FIRST COMMERCIAL INTERCONTINENTAL AIRPORT

IN COMMEMORATION OF THE AIRPORT'S ROLE
IN PIONEERING INTERNATIONAL AIR TRAVEL

K.L.M.	LISBON	NOV 1944
BRITISH OVERSEAS AIRWAYS CORP.	SYDNEY	MAY 1945
AMERICAN AIRLINES (Flagship London)	**NEW YORK**	**OCT 1945**
PAN AMERICAN WORLD	NEW YORK	OCT 1945
SOUTH AFRICAN AIRWAYS	JOHANNESBURG	NOV 1945

THIS PLAQUE COMMEMORATES THE 50th ANNIVERSARY OF THE FIRST EVER SCHEDULED
LANDPLANE TRANSATLANTIC PASSENGER FLIGHT, FROM NEW YORK TO HURN BY
AMERICAN AIRLINES DC4 ON THE 24th OCTOBER 1945.
FLIGHT TIME 14 HOURS 5 MINUTES

The first transatlantic scheduled landplane service was operated by American Airlines with a Douglas DC-4 from New York to Bournemouth, arriving on 24 October 1945. This historic event is commemorated by a plaque situated by the public enclosure of the terminal building.

Passengers disembarking from the first American Airlines Douglas DC-4 flight from New York, NC90901, having made a refuelling stop at Shannon. Pan American World Airways first scheduled service arrived four days later.

Major overhauls being carried out on Avro Yorks by BOAC No.2 Maintenance Line in their hangars on the north side of the airport. Their wingspan exceeded the width of the hangar door and so they had to be pulled in sideways on special dollies guided by rails in the floor.

The BOAC Lancastrians received modified markings by 1947, with smaller registrations, a prominent Speedbird on the nose, and the RAF fin flashes replaced by a Union Jack. The majority of the fleet only had an active service life of just over three years.

A job well done! Maintenance crews from BOAC's No.2 Maintenance Line pose with an Avro York that has just completed an overhaul. *Montrose* was delivered to Bournemouth in the summer of 1946 and sports a shining metal finish, plus BOAC's familiar Speedbird logo.

The BOAC Development Flight tested a number of new airliners and engines. Having ordered a fleet of Handley Page Hermes IVs in the spring of 1947, BOAC tested the earlier tailwheel Hermes II G-AGUB in the spring of 1949 before receiving the production version in 1950.

BOAC pinned it's post-war hopes on a large fleet of Avro Tudors. Their flagship *Elizabeth of England* was named by Princess Elizabeth in 1947, but never flew a service before being sold to BSAA. Operated for only two years, it then joined others in storage at Bournemouth.

Staff and aircrew of the BOAC Development Flight outside the Flight's hangar on the north side of the airport during 1949. It was one of two similar hangars completed for BOAC during 1946 to cope with their growing fleet.

BOAC operated a large fleet of Avro Yorks to destinations in Egypt, the Middle East and South Africa. With the return to peace the fleet soon appeared in natural silver, although G-AGJC was experimentally painted dark blue in 1949.

Qantas had operated Lancastrians jointly with BOAC on the Sydney service, but acquired a fleet of Lockheed Constellations in 1947 to replace them. The first is seen at Bournemouth on a proving flight in November, the aircraft being fitted with an under fuselage luggage pannier.

31

BOAC did not only have airliners based at Bournemouth, but also operated the Speedbird Flying Club for its staff. Two of their Hawk Trainers are seen outside the terminal area in 1949, while other aircraft with the Club included Austers and Tiger Moths.

The initial Handley Page Hermes IVs were delivered to BOAC early in 1950 in natural metal finish, although later ones were painted with white cabin tops and a blue cheat line. G-ALDG is crew training during 1950, and its fuselage is currently preserved at Duxford.

During the late 1940s, aircraft from the world's major airlines were to be seen at Bournemouth at times of fog in the London area. Brand new Convair 240 OO-AWS of the Belgium airline Sabena was one such arrival in November 1949.

Another diversion has brought Douglas DC-4 LN-IAE of Scandinavian Airlines System from London Airport. Note the SAS pennant above the cockpit and passengers on the ground having disembarked from another aircraft – hopefully under control.

A major event in 1950 was the South Coast Air Race held in September, with aircraft flying along the South Coast to a finishing point at Herne Bay, Kent. Aircraft ranged in size from Comper Swifts to a Handley Page Halifax VIII G-AKEC, which is seen prior to the Race.

A view of the Control Tower in the early 1960s. Its wartime look is still retained, but now with the 1953 octagonal glass tower added to the top of the veranda that had originally been used for watching movements. Its earlier layout can be seen in the previous photograph.

Airspeed built the graceful Ambassador airliner at nearby Christchurch, but undertook much test flying from the hard runways at Bournemouth. Here the prototype lifts off from runway 08 at its intersection with the cross runway.

The first sustained scheduled services to the Channel Islands were operated by Jersey Airlines from the summer of 1952. Seen in front of the terminal area is one of their fleet of Dragon Rapides, which were later replaced by Herons and Dakotas.

Bournemouth received the first visit of a jet airliner as early as November 1949, when the prototype de Havilland Comet visited the BOAC Development Flight. Comet 1s were seen crew training during 1952/53, plus, as on this occasion, during diversions from London.

Having first seen the Douglas airliners of Pan American World in 1945, the airport continued to see them during the 1950s. *Clipper Fidelity* is a Douglas DC-6B diverted from London Airport in March 1953, and Pan American were last seen on such diversions in 1958.

Regular visitors during the mid-1950s for crew training were BOAC's fleet of Canadair Argonauts. Powered by Rolls Royce Merlins, their noise did not enamour them to the local residents. Seen under the tail of G-ALHF is the wartime VIP hangar.

Normally crew training in the 1950s would be undertaken by BOAC aircraft flying down from London Airport. However from 1956 there were always two Britannia's based at the airport, proving themselves to being quieter than other airliners, hence the Whispering Giant name.

Jersey Airlines introduced Dakotas in May 1959, the first routes being those from Jersey to Bournemouth and London. In service they were known as Dakmasters. Here G-AMYJ is refuelled while parked on the grass in front of the terminal during the summer of 1960.

At the time, charter flights from Bournemouth were rare, but this 1960 view shows the staff of local store J.J. Allen looking forward to their flight to Paris aboard Vickers Viking G-AJBX of Maitland Drewery Aviation.

Air Safaris commenced scheduled services from Bournemouth with Vikings in April 1961. G-AHOW has just returned on the early evening flight from Ostend, but all services ceased abruptly in September when the airline went out of business.

In the early 1960s IT holiday flights to Palma on behalf of Bath Travel were operated by Airspeed Ambassadors of Dan-Air London. The airline also operated a holiday service from Bristol to Basle, calling at Bournemouth.

Having originally been seen at the airport in 1947 when in service with BOAC, Lockheed Constellation G-AHEJ returned in January 1961 for service with Falcon Airways. Falcon had operated Vikings from Bournemouth, but the Constellation was to be based at Gatwick.

Jersey Airlines took a great step forward with the introduction of a fleet of Handley Page Dart Heralds in 1961. However the airline merged into the British United Group in May 1962, and their titles had replaced those of Jersey by the following summer.

The wartime buildings still in use as the passenger terminal were expanded with this wooden extension in 1960 to cope with additional business. This included Silver City's cross channel air ferry service for cars and passengers. Bicycles were also carried for the sum of 5s.

A view from airside of the terminal buildings in the 1960s with a 'temporary' new passenger lounge to the left and remaining wartime buildings, with later additions, to the right. A small public enclosure was also provided.

Passengers waiting for their flight outside of the terminal area in the summer of 1965. Beyond was the public enclosure with wartime wooden huts still in use, and in the distance is the College of Air Traffic Control. Pleasure flights were available in a Dragon Rapide.

Inside the main passenger terminal in the summer of 1965 – although it could almost be the 1930s. Housed in extended wartime buildings, it was another fifteen years before work started on a new terminal for the airport.

Silver City operated cross channel car ferry services to Cherbourg and the Channel Islands with Bristol Superfreighters. Parked in the snow during the winter of 1963, G-ANWM was soon to gain British United titles as Silver City had become part of the Group in January 1962.

Diverted from Heathrow on 29 December 1961, Sud Caravelle VIN I-DABA of Alitalia was the first of the type to be seen at Bournemouth. In later years Caravelles of Swissair operated charters from Zurich with students for local language colleges.

The airport was sold by the Board of Trade to Bournemouth and Dorset Councils on 1 April 1969. Alderman Michael Green, Chairman of the Airport's Management Committee, awaits the handover of the official licence documents from William Rogers, the Minister of State.

Harry Longhurst was appointed Airport Director in April 1969, a post that he was to hold for twenty-three years – much longer than he had anticipated. Tie off and hard at work on paperwork in 1978, Harry did much to promote the airport and boost traffic in the early days.

As well as being produced locally, Vickers Viscounts were used by many airlines over the years, mainly on services to the Channel Islands. G-APND of British United is seen returning from such a flight, other airlines included BEA, Cambrian, Channel and Dan-Air.

Day trips to the Dutch bulb fields have always proved popular, here Invicta Airways Douglas DC-4 G-ASPM is about to depart for Rotterdam in the spring of 1966. Many European capitals and cities are presently served by daytrips provided by Palmair.

The summer of 1972 saw Operation Redskin – the airlift of tomatoes from Guernsey to Bournemouth. To assist the Dakotas normally used on the service three Argosies of Sagittair, plus a civilian Hercules, were brought in to assist due to their much greater payload.

The early days of locally-based freight airline Channel Express. Guernsey flowers handled by Express Air Freight are unloaded from Douglas Dakota G-AMPY during the summer of 1977. Express operated its own aircraft the following year, becoming Channel Express in 1982.

Bournemouth's first Boeing 707 was Wardair of Canada's CF-ZYP diverted from Gatwick on 11 January 1971. Considered to be a large aircraft for the airport at the time, others appeared infrequently over the years, along with a few Douglas DC-8s.

Seeming almost as large as a Boeing 707, Convair Coronados of Spanish charter airline Spantax were used for holiday flights to Majorca from the spring of 1968. They looked most impressive on take off, with much noise and exhaust smoke coming from their engines.

Dan-Air operated Hawker Siddeley 748s on its scheduled services from Bournemouth in the 1970/80s. These were to the Channel Islands and northwards to Manchester and Newcastle. The opportunity is being taken to advertise other flights from Bournemouth (Hurn) Airport.

Turnround activity for Dan-Air's de Havilland Comet 4C G-BDIX. Mobile steps to the left, GPU at the nose and Shell refueller to the right. The Comet's front crew door was situated on the starboard side, as opposed to the more normal port side these days.

Diversions due to Air Traffic Control strikes in London during May 1981 made Bournemouth look like a real international airport. This selection of tails includes British Airways One-Eleven and Tridents, Lufthansa Boeing 727 and SAS Douglas DC-9.

As well as operating HS.748s for Channel Island services, Dan-Air used Comet 4s for many holiday flights in the 1970/80s. Palmair passengers bound for Majorca are seen boarding during the summer of 1978.

Freddie Laker brought his brand new DC-10 G-AZZC to Bournemouth on 15 December 1971 whilst on a round-country tour. Later some of his Skytrain services appeared on diversions from Gatwick.

SAS Airbus A.300s were also included in the May 1981 ATC diversions from Heathrow. However they caused problems, as it was found that the top rung of the airport's mobile steps were eighteen inches below the aircraft's doors. Great care was needed by the SAS hostesses.

Among the more unusual aircraft to be diverted from Gatwick was this Canadair CL-44D freighter HB-IEN of Transvalair, which appeared on 21 November 1979. At least there wasn't the worry of transporting the passengers to London!

Again a diversion due to strikes at London, as opposed to the normal bad weather. Here passengers disembark from Lufthansa Boeing 737 D-ABFM in June 1981 prior to finishing their journey by road, hopefully not all the way by the corporation bus.

During the summer months Dan-Air frequently needed extra capacity to help on its Channel Island services, which were normally operated by HS.748s. Sometimes their own Viscounts were used and others were chartered, such as G-CSZA from Southern International in 1979.

Following the retirement of their Comet fleet in 1980, Dan-Air used Boeing 727s for their holiday flights, as they had the advantage of greater capacity and range. They were also seen on diversions from Dan-Air's main base at Gatwick.

The airport's cargo hangar, close to the terminal, was originally the wartime VIP one. This 1983 view shows flowers, unloaded from a Channel Express Dart Herald, about to depart for London markets onboard a refrigerated trailer unit.

The Airport Fire Service always liked to have an old aircraft to play with, and during the 1980s they were able to use the fuselage of a time-expired Boeing 707. Here it is being well covered in foam during an exercise by *Thunderbird 2*.

From the beginning of 1978 the majority of the Channel Islands' freight traffic has been carried by locally based Channel Express. Their fleet of Handley Page Dart Heralds and Fokker F-27s have proved well suited, as their low door sill height has aided loading and unloading.

In 1990 Channel Express introduced a fleet of Lockheed Electra freighters into service on their Channel Island routes. Following the expansion of their overnight parcels business, the Electras were then used on European routes, being seen less frequently at Bournemouth.

Diverted from Gatwick in February 1991, Boeing 757 G-OOOH of Air 2000 was the first passenger carrying airliner to arrive at Bournemouth direct from America since the propeller era diversions of the 1950s. It was returning holidaymakers from Orlando in Florida.

Whilst undertaking a round the country flight in 1991, the crew of this Solar Wings Pegasus Quasar microlight stopped off at the airport to refuel and stretch their legs. The charity flight was sponsored by Jersey European who operated services to the Channel Islands at the time.

Euro Direct Airlines was launched in the spring of 1994, with a fleet of BAe Jetstream 31s and BAe ATPs. Services were operated to various European destinations, but unfortunately the airline ceased operations in less than twelve months.

Farewell to the Vickers Viscount. In recognition of the many built at Bournemouth, and also the airport's use by many Viscount operators, a special flight was arranged with G-APEY on 30 November 1997 to mark the type's end of passenger service operations in the UK.

Memories of an old timer. At the start of a European Tour to commemorate the Berlin Air Lift, this preserved C-121 Constellation in USAF MATS colours, stayed a few days in May 1998, recalling days fifty years before of Air India, American, BOAC, Pan American and Qantas.

The visit of the preserved Constellation N494TW taught the Shell tanker driver some old tricks. The piston engine airliner required overwing refuelling, with the pilot checking the fuel tank levels by dip stick. Those were the days!

Three

Military Activity

Following its adoption as a civil airport, military traffic at Bournemouth was mainly limited to RAF transports – Ansons, Oxfords and Valettas, with the odd Lancaster or Lincoln. The airport had to wait until 1951 for the return of any based military activity when one of the former BOAC hangars was taken over by Airwork Services for their Fleet Requirement Unit, which operated fighters acting as 'targets' for naval gunners on exercise in the English Channel. Operations commenced in June 1952 with Sea Mosquitoes, followed by Sea Hornets. From the summer of 1953 Airwork also operated a number of Oxfords on behalf of the radar station at nearby RAF Sopley, here the aircraft acting as 'target blips' for trainee plotters. The Sea Hornets lasted until October 1955 when they were replaced by Sea Furies and Attackers, with the first of many Sea Hawks arriving in January 1957. The Sea Hawks soon received an all over black colour scheme to make them more visible 'targets', as well as having a searchlight fitted in their underwing fuel tank. At the same time Fireflies were received as target tugs – the naval gunners now having something they could hit. They only lasted a short time, being replaced by Meteor TT.20s in May 1958, the FRU being the first operator of this new mark. June 1957 saw the arrival of Balliols which were operated by Airwork for four years on behalf of the School of Fighter Control, which had just moved into RAF Sopley. As with the Oxfords, these were flown on behalf of the trainee plotters and trackers, with the aircraft normally operating in pairs.

Another BOAC hangar was taken over by de Havilland Aircraft, who were already using the airport for trials with the Ambassador airliner. The hangar was used as a production flight test base for the jets de Havilland were building at nearby Christchurch, which at the time only had a grass runway. Vampire trainers appeared from the spring of 1952, with Sea Vampires, Venoms and Sea Venoms the following year. The prototype Sea Vixen, then still referred to as DH.110 Mk.20X, landed at the end of its maiden flight in June 1955, although it was the spring of 1957 before production aircraft began to appear. Due to complaints about noise, the majority of de Havilland test flying was transferred to their main base at Hatfield in July 1959.

The airport was used to give air experience flights to local ATC and CCF cadets, with types used during the 1950/1960s being Ansons, Chipmunks and Oxfords. Other aircraft called to clear customs whilst inbound/outbound of the country, examples being Belgium AF Dakotas and C-119 Packets en route to Tarrant Rushton, French AF Flaments and Noratlas', RCAF Beech 18s, USAF C-47s and aircraft from A & AEE at Boscombe Down ranging from Balliols to Hastings. The late fifties saw an increase in RAF crew training – including Varsities from Thorney Island, Britannias and Comets from Lyneham, with the first Hercules appearing in the autumn of 1967.

Airwork Services were responsible for the delivery of aircraft to a number of foreign air arms. During 1960/1961 sixteen Gannets for the Indonesian Navy passed through Bournemouth, followed by Jet Provosts for Sudan in 1963/64, Beavers for the South Arabian Air Force in 1967, and Caribous for Abu Dhabi in 1969. A major contract was awarded to Airwork Services by the Royal Saudi Air Force in 1966 for support and training, resulting in a number of their aircraft being seen, commencing with Hunters in May. There was a similar contract awarded by the Sultan of Oman Air Force in 1968, with Dakotas and Strikemasters passing through by the end of the year. These were followed by Viscounts, Caribous, Islanders and Skyvans, continuing until the spring of 1990 with the final Skyvan overhaul.

The final Sea Furies were taken out of service with the Airwork FRU in May 1962, at which time there were fourteen Sea Hawks in service, plus four Meteors. A replacement for the Sea Hawk arrived in December 1965 with the first of many Scimitars. The heavy fighter was not really suited to the job, being more complex than the Sea Hawks and requiring additional maintenance, so it was decided to replace them with Hunter GA.11s – the first arriving in March 1969. The final Scimitar did not depart until February 1971, being the last ever flight by a Scimitar. The Meteor target tugs were also replaced, with the first Canberra TT.18 being received in September 1969. As well as operating for the Royal Navy around the British coast, the FRU aircraft often flew down to Gibraltar to take part in fleet exercises held in the Mediterranean. Local activity ceased in October 1972 when the Canberras and Hunters were transferred to Yeovilton to join their existing Sea Vixens in forming the FRADU.

The Red Arrows Gnats were first seen in August 1971 in connection with their display over Bournemouth Seafront, becoming regular summer visitors, frequently using Bournemouth as a base for displays elsewhere. Their replacement Hawks were first seen at the Air Pageant in July 1980, and the team marked its twenty-first anniversary in May 1986 at Bournemouth's Air Show. December 1978 saw the arrival from Hamble of the Bulldogs of Southampton University Air Squadron and the Chipmunks of No.2 Air Experience Flight. Both had put up with waterlogged grass runways at Hamble for long enough, but the Bulldogs found the weekday airspace around Bournemouth rather crowded and so later moved to Lee-on-Solent. The Chipmunks continued to provide flights to ATC and CCF cadets until March 1996 when the trainers were retired from RAF service – the cadets then having to travel to Boscombe Down for flights.

The late 1990s saw a decline in military activity – the RAF possessing less aircraft. A reduction in their Hercules fleet saw less crew training undertaken from Lyneham, although Chinooks from Odiham were frequent. Bournemouth still sees visits by aircraft from all three services.

The Airwork-operated Fleet Requirement Unit initially operated Sea Mosquitoes and Sea Hornets, before being replaced by Sea Furies in 1955. Here FB.11 WJ288 is topped up from the wartime vintage fuel bowser. WJ288 was later to be preserved at Southend.

The Airwork FRU received the first of a large number of Hawker Sea Hawks in January 1957, replacing the earlier Supermarine Attackers. Initially they were operated in standard Royal Navy colours, but were soon painted black to make them more visible.

First jets with the FRU were Supermarine Attacker FB.2s. However this is WK328 of 890 Squadron parked close to the tower during a visit to the airport in 1952. Six of the fighters served with the FRU from 1954 until 1958.

Target towing duties at the FRU were undertaken from 1957 by a handful of Firefly TT.4s until replaced by Meteors in the following year. TW723 receives attention from the ground crews, its ML winch being mounted under its forward fuselage.

De Havilland maintained a flight test hangar on the north side of the airfield for the fighters built at nearby Christchurch, which only had a grass runway. Seen landing after an early test flight is the prototype Sea Vixen XF828, still referred to as the DH.110 Mk.20X at the time.

During 1960/1961, Airwork Services arranged the delivery of fourteen Gannet AS.4s to the Angk Laut (Indonesian Navy). On a typically British flying day, the delivery crew for two of the Gannets prepare to depart Bournemouth on the long flight eastwards.

The Fleet Requirement Unit's early Firefly target tugs were replaced by Gloster Meteor TT.20s from May 1958. Further aircraft were received from Hal Far, Malta, when the base closed, and WD785 is seen here on arrival at Bournemouth in April 1967.

Hawker Hunter GA.11s operated with the Fleet Requirement Unit from March 1969 until the Unit moved to Yeovilton in October 1972. To help pilot familiarization, a Hunter T.8 was borrowed from Brawdy for a few months, here being refuelled outside the FRU hangar.

Early in 1961 six dismantled Percival Provosts arrived at Airwork Services, with five of them eventually being scrapped. However one was soon put to use for a Civil Defence exercise held in Poole in March 1961. Luckily the locals had been forewarned that it was not a crash.

Airwork Services obtained a contract in 1966 to provide support and training to the Royal Saudi Air Force. This included the supply of eight Cessna 172s for initial training, with 616 seen awaiting delivery in April 1968.

Airwork's Saudi contract was soon followed by a similar one for the Sultan of Oman Air Force. What choice could there be for initial transports for this new Air Force other than the Douglas C-47 – here 502 awaits delivery in August 1969.

The Sultan of Oman Air Force chose the de Havilland Canada Caribou as a tactical transport, and the first of three stopped off in 1969 whilst on its delivery flight. Other transports seen for Oman were Skyvans and Islanders.

Various BAC Strikemasters passed through the airport on delivery during the late sixties and early seventies. Four for the South Yemen Air Force stopped off in August 1969, with other recipients including Oman and Singapore.

The French have always been well represented by a variety of transports passing through, usually clearing customs. The 1960s-1970s saw the likes of Air Force Breguet Saharas, Dassault Flaments and Nord Noratlases. In later years the Noratlases appeared on training flights.

The French Navy have also helped to boost visitors to the airport, again usually clearing customs. Types have included Falcon 10s, Nord 262s, Piper Navajos, and, coming up to date, Embraer Xingus. Here MS Paris 85 has arrived from Landivisiau in December 1993.

The Airport Director, Harry Longhurst, fancies his chances as a fighter pilot. Seen inside the wartime VIP hangar is BoBMF Supermarine Spitfire AB910 which visited in November 1969 to take part in a local Remembrance Day flypast.

De Havilland Chipmunks of No.2 Air Experience Flight were based at the airport from December 1978 until their withdrawal from RAF service in March 1996. The Flight's four aircraft are here being examined by local Air Training Corps (ATC) cadets.

From time to time medical emergency flights operate into the airport, usually by civilian aircraft. However in February 1994 such duties were being carried out by a Luftwaffe VFW.614 17+02, with attendant ambulance.

Over the years a variety of military aircraft have called at Bournemouth. The US Navy Convair VC-131 was fairly unusual in itself, but is framed by the tail of much rarer Algerian Air Force Antonov An-12 serial 566 in September 1981.

Lockheed Hercules of many operators have passed through the airport. One of the more frequent is the United Arab Emirates Air Force, who operate the stretched version of the Hercules, with 311 seen parked amongst various bollards while the apron is repaired.

The Avro Vulcan V-jet bomber was always a firm favourite with Air Show devotees, and here makes a sprightly take off during the 1988 Show. It last appeared at the airport in 1990, unless *Vulcan to the Sky* can change this.

Air Shows naturally bring various military visitors. At the 1991 Show this 74 Squadron McDonnell Phantom FGR.2 XV401 carried a 'For Sale' sign on its intake, indicating the impending withdrawal of Phantoms from RAF service.

The 1991 Air Show was titled 'Back from the Gulf' and included this weary looking Buccaneer S.2 XX885 *Sky Pirate* in pink camouflage. Operational problems meant that 1991 was to be the last show held at the airport.

The last Buccaneer to be seen at the airport was XX897 which flew in from Bedford in August 1993. Eventually it ended up as an engine test bed for the Quicksilver world water speed record boat, taxiing again early in 1999.

US Navy visitors to be seen over the years have included Beech C-12, Douglas C-9s (seen here is one from VR-58 squadron), Lockheed Hercules and VP-3 Orions. These visits are usually bringing 'Navy Brass' to visit the nearby Naval Bases at Portland and Portsmouth.

Parked with their support Lockheed Hercules, the Red Arrows BAe Hawks are seen outside the Bournemouth Flying Club in September 1989 during a visit to mark the twenty-fifth anniversary of the Red Arrows, whose pilots were honorary members of the Club.

The Flying Club has attracted various military types over the years. This TTTE Tornado GR.1 from Cottesmore called on 7 November 1995 so that the crew could give a talk to the club members. Other visitors to their hangars have included a Hawk and Sea Harrier.

BAe Nimrod MR.2 XV246 visited in March 2001 while on an exercise, and others appear from Kinloss to undertake ILS runs while on training flights. All current RAF and RN types can be seen, although less frequently than in the past.

Four

Vickers-Armstrongs & BAC

In June 1951 Vickers-Armstrongs of Weybridge took over one of BOAC's hangars for flight test work whilst a hard runway was being laid at their Wisley airfield. This brought the brand new Valiant V-bomber to Bournemouth for its early flight trials, as well as the Viscount airliner prototypes. At the time Vickers had a full production line of Valettas and Varsity trainers at Weybridge, with priority production of the Valiant to follow. Orders were being received for the Viscount, and, needing to increase production capacity, it was decided to expand the Bournemouth site to undertake Varsity production. Initially only wings and tails were built, with fuselages coming down from Weybridge. The first aircraft was completed in November 1951, with production continuing for the next two years. Regrettably the Valiant prototype was lost on 12 January 1952 following a severe engine fire whilst on a test flight over the south coast. Many people remember it flying high over the town with flames pouring from the engine, desperately trying to lose height in order to land back at the airport, but the crew were forced to abandon the bomber just before it blew up, coming down at nearby Bransgore with the loss of the co-pilot's life. Flight testing moved back to Wisley in 1952, but by then Vickers had decided that the Viscount would also be built at Bournemouth. The first began to take shape during the summer of 1953, by which time Vickers had doubled the hangar space to give two parallel production lines. Initially Series 700 aircraft were built at Weybridge, which moved on the larger Series 800 in 1956. Bournemouth took over all the Series 700 production, moving on to the Series 800 in 1958, with fuselages also being built for Weybridge. The first Bournemouth-built aircraft flew in December 1953, and by the autumn of 1954 two Viscounts a week were being delivered, a huge boost being received in August when Capital Airlines of Washington placed an order for thirty, later to be doubled. This involved the design office in much additional work to prepare the airliner for service in North America. When Viscount production slowed down, overhaul work was undertaken on RAF Valiants and Varsities from 1959 – the Valiant modification programme lasting for four years.

The British Aircraft Corporation was formed on 1 July 1960, with Vickers-Armstrongs (Aircraft) Ltd being one of its major components, along with English Electric, Bristol Aircraft and Hunting Aircraft. In April 1961 BAC announced the One-Eleven airliner, setting up design offices at Bournemouth and Weybridge, with final assembly at Bournemouth. This was followed in May by the first order for ten by British United, with an all important order for six from Braniff of America in October. The prototype One-Eleven was rolled out in July 1963, interestingly with the hangars still bearing Vickers-Armstrongs (Aircraft) Ltd titles. The maiden flight was on the evening of 20 August, with large crowds of local residents viewing from the adjacent road. After a couple of weeks the One-Eleven flew to Wisley which was designated the flight test base, and it was from there that it took off on a test flight on 22 October, during which it entered a deep stall from which it could not recover. The aircraft crashed at Chicklade, Wiltshire, killing the test crew, the news bringing a stunned silence to the Bournemouth site. The reason for the stall was soon recognized, and production for British United continued. The final day of the year saw the name Vickers-Armstrongs officially disappear – it was now British Aircraft Corporation (Operating) Ltd, the Bournemouth site being part of the Weybridge Division.

The One-Eleven entered service with British United and Braniff in April 1965, and the first of a major order from American Airlines was delivered at the end of December. The lengthened One-Eleven 500 first flew in June 1967, being a rebuild of one of the earlier development aircraft, the new version being ordered by BEA. Other work included the building of Concorde noses for Filton, Jet Provost and Strikemaster wings for the Preston assembly line, plus the overhaul of Pembrokes, Sea Princes and Viscounts. BEA's first One-Eleven 500 was delivered in 1968, with others following for British United and Caledonian. Another version was the short field 475, the prototype being the rebuilt – and shortened – 500 prototype, flying in August 1970.

The One-Eleven was a noisy airliner, and BAC and Rolls Royce developed a 'hush kit' to reduce the noise, being flight tested in June 1974 and offering some benefit. To meet a Japanese short field requirement, the series 670 was proposed, with the prototype 475 being converted yet again in 1977 as the development aircraft, but the order was not forthcoming. From 1 January 1978 the British Aircraft Corporation became part of British Aerospace, having merged with the Hawker Siddeley Group. The following June saw the signing of the 'Rombac Deal' where One-Elevens would be produced in Romania, initial planning being for twenty-five aircraft, with the Romanians completing three aircraft at Bournemouth. The first of these flew at the end of 1980, and the first completed in Bucharest flew in August 1982.

A bombshell came on 6 July 1983 when British Aerospace announced that the Bournemouth site would be closed the following year 'due to the depressed state of the worldwide civil aircraft market'. There was hardly any One-Eleven work, and possible sub-contract work on the proposed Airbus A.320 did not materialize due to delays in launching the airliner. One of the remaining One-Elevens was registered G-BLHD to denote 'Last Hurn Delivery', departing in May 1984. The site became deserted by the autumn, but did not suffer the indignity of being demolished, as by the following spring three quarters of the site had been re-let to other firms.

Between 1951 and 1981 Bournemouth saw the production by Vickers and BAC of 146 Varsity trainers, 279 Viscount airliners, 220 One-Eleven airliners, the final assembly of ten Strikemaster trainers as well as the overhaul of Valiant bombers – a substantial portion of Britain's post-war aircraft production.

Vickers-Armstrongs set up a flight test base on the north side of the airport in 1951, and an early visitor was the prototype Vickers Viscount airliner, here carrying BEA titles. The Tay-powered jet Viscount was also based at Bournemouth during the summer.

The early days of Varsity trainer production for the RAF at Bournemouth in the summer of 1951. In a rather deserted hangar, their fuselages have arrived by road from Weybridge and await fitment of the locally produced wings and tails.

Opposite below: The first Vickers Viscount for Capital Airlines N4702 prior to delivery in June 1955. Sixty were ordered, but the final ones remained undelivered at the end of 1957 as the airline had run into financial difficulties and were unable to pay for them.

The first Vickers Viscount 700s on the production line during the summer of 1953. The Dart engines are being fitted to BEA's first aircraft G-AMOO, which was completed in December. The hangar is one of those previously used by BOAC's No.2 Maintenance Line.

The Vickers VC.10 had some parts made locally, but was built at Weybridge and test flown from Wisley. Seen outside the Bournemouth factory is early production aircraft G-ARVC, which made a rare visit in March 1963 so that the local workforce could see the finished product.

Piloted by Jock Bryce, the BAC One-Eleven prototype G-ASHG returns to Bournemouth at the end of its maiden flight on the evening of 20 August 1963. The Jet Provost has been acting as chase aircraft during the flight.

The first export order for the BAC One-Eleven was from Braniff Airways in October 1961. N1543 was the first to be delivered to their Dallas base in March 1965, entering service the following month – the same time that those for British United entered service from Gatwick.

Early stages in the production of the BAC One-Eleven. Forward and centre fuselage sections were made locally, with parts made at Filton, Luton and Weybridge being brought together at Bournemouth for final assembly.

The One-Eleven Srs.500 entered service with BEA in September 1968. The type also proved popular with German charter airlines, with Germanair's D-AMOR outside the BAC flight shed early in February 1970.

The British Aircraft Corporation factory at Bournemouth was also involved in the production of the supersonic BAC Concorde airliner. The droop noses were built during 1974 – these parts being for an Air France aircraft.

The BAC factory also undertook the overhaul of aircraft in the 1970s, including Hunting Percival Sea Princes which had previously received attention at the now closed Luton factory. In September 1971 WP308 awaits return to the Royal Navy.

Vickers Viscounts also returned to the BAC factory in the 1970s for overhaul. Just visible on this Sultan of Oman Air Force aircraft is the slipper fuel tank outboard of the engines – this being a rarely used option for Viscount operators.

The 'Rombac' deal of June 1978 brought a number of freighters to the airport. Seen arriving from Romania, this Tarom Antonov An-26 has called to collect One-Eleven jigs for the new production line to be set up in Bucharest. Tarom Boeing 707s were also used to collect parts.

To set up the Romanian production line, three complete fuselages were built at Bournemouth and flown out to Bucharest during 1981. The first left in April on board a Super Guppy freighter supplied by Airbus Industries – the swing nose giving a clear run for the fuselage.

Work under way on ten Strikemasters in the summer of 1980. The unassembled aircraft were brought down from Warton for completion at Bournemouth. The first flew as G-16-26 in August, later appearing in Sudan AF colours, although it was eventually delivered to Ecuador.

The closure of the British Aerospace factory in the summer of 1984 did not mean the end of One-Elevens at Hurn. The hangars passed to Lovaux who undertook airliner overhaul work – mainly on One-Elevens. This summer 1992 view shows aircraft of Ryanair and Okada.

Five

FR Aviation

With the impending closure of Tarrant Rushton, Flight Refuelling's Airfield Division took up residence in one hangar at Bournemouth in June 1979. Renamed the Aircraft Operating Division, it was mainly involved in the development of the Sea Vixen as a pilotless drone, but it was not anticipated that the work would occupy them for very long. So Bournemouth was regarded as just a short-term site, with a staff of only thirty-six. Work on the Sea Vixen drones progressed slowly and in the autumn of 1983 the MOD suspended further work due to costs. Flight Refuelling took over the overhaul and maintenance of the Flight Systems' F-100F Super Sabres, following the closure of British Aerospace, when they also submitted a proposal for a drone version to cover the cancelled Sea Vixen. There were also visits by Cessna 441 and Mitsubishi Mu-2 aircraft of SwedAir, who used them as 'lightweight' target tugs on behalf of the Swedish Air Force.

Following the Falklands War of 1982 a team from Flight Refuelling studied what lessons the Royal Navy could learn in the line of aerial defence. At the time, their training was undertaken from Yeovilton with Hunters acting as targets and Canberras as target tugs. The study concluded that more up to date targets were needed and that there was a more cost effective way of target towing. This study was to change the future of the company. Trials using the SwedAir aircraft showed that although not as fast as Canberras, they were much cheaper to operate and their sleeve targets more reliable. It was decided that an executive jet would be more appropriate – being faster and able to carry more equipment. Flight Refuelling selected the Falcon 20 as it retained the basic wing of the Mystere fighter and was capable of carrying a large amount of underwing stores. Pods containing various electronic jammers were carried, along with others containing towed targets – some of which could be trailed six miles behind the aircraft. Flight Refuelling's proposals were accepted and they were awarded the contract to operate future FRADU training. In January 1985 Flight Refuelling formed a new company to handle the contract – FR Aviation. Ten Falcon 20s were acquired, the first arriving in January before moving to Yeovilton to commence the new Electronic Warfare and Threat Simulation role. Initially they acted in the EW role acting as attacking aircraft, but with updates to the pods they later became 'missiles'. Early in 1986 a new hangar and large apron area was constructed at Bournemouth for Falcon operations, the aircraft returning from Yeovilton in May, with the fleet peaking at twenty-two. In 1995 a second base was opened at Teesside Airport to support nine Falcons following FR Aviation obtaining the RAF electronic warfare contract.

In another development, Flight Refuelling had been involved in trials with an Islander to study its suitability for inshore fisheries surveillance duties. The company was awarded a contract by the MAFF, commencing operations with their own Islander in September 1982. Following experience with the Fisheries Patrol contract, FR Aviation studied other aircraft that would give greater operational flexibility. A Dornier 228 was demonstrated at Bournemouth in August 1985, and when the contract was renewed in September 1986 two Dorniers were ordered to supplement the Islander. Introduction of the Dorniers meant that RAF Nimrods could be released from this type of maritime duty, the Dorniers being fitted with enhanced electronics and an under fuselage 360° search radar. More recent contracts continue to see the Dorniers employed on aerial surveillance duties.

FR Aviation obtained a contract in 1989 for the major servicing of RAF Canberras, with the first arriving in April. Initially granted for a five year period, the contract kept being extended, with the small remaining fleet of PR.9s still being serviced at the present time. This was followed in January 1990 by a contract for the conversion of eight RAF transport VC.10s into dual purpose tanker/transports. With the increase in this new overhaul business, a large hangar was erected for the purpose, being opened in February 1991. Following the conversion of the initial VC.10s in June 1992, FR Aviation received an additional contract covering the RAF's remaining five aircraft. In all, the contracts were worth about £60 million, and made FR Aviation one of the major employers in the area.

In July 1996 British Aerospace obtained the contract to rework the RAF's fleet of Nimrod MR.2s under the Nimrod 2000 Project. FR Aviation was the prime sub-contractor for rebuilding the airframes, prior to delivering them to BAe for fitting out. Once again another large hangar was constructed for the conversion work, being completed in the winter of 1998. The fuselage of the first Nimrod was flown in from Kinloss in February 1997 inside a Russian An-124 freighter – the RAF having no suitable transports. In November 1999 BAe announced that it was taking the whole project back in house, resulting in four part converted fuselages being flown out by An-124.

Third party maintenance work expanded, now seeing such types as Boeing 727s, Falcon executive jets, BAC One-Elevens and Short 360s. One Canberra attended to in the spring of 1999 was interesting as it was returned to the RAF painted as the prototype VN799 for display at Air Shows to mark the fiftieth anniversary of the Canberra's first flight in 1949. Also undertaken were major overhauls and re-engining of airline and executive Boeing 727s, plus major overhauls of BAe.146s.

December 2001 saw the setting up of a new company – Bournemouth Aerospace Engineering – jointly owned by FR Aviation and Singapore Technologies Aerospace, to undertake airliner maintenance and overhaul work. In addition to this, FRA is part of the Air Tanker consortium bidding for the RAF's Future Strategic Tanker Aircraft – other major members being EADS, Rolls-Royce and Thales. The consortium propose a modified Airbus A.330 airliner as a replacement tanker/transport for the RAF.

The FR Aviation fleet of Dassault Falcon 20s are some of the most active aircraft at Bournemouth. Initially they were operated on the American register, and here N904FR is in formation with Phantom FGR.2s of 56 Squadron during air defence training in 1990.

When Flight Refuelling arrived from Tarrant Rushton in June 1979 they brought with them the Sea Vixen target drone project. Squeezed into their new hangar are the four aircraft involved in the development program, which was cancelled in the autumn of 1983.

During the 1980s, Flight Refuelling maintained six former Danish Air Force F-100F Super Sabres on behalf of Flight Systems Inc. (later Tracor) of the USA. The aircraft operated with the USAF in Europe, acting as target tugs for high-speed drogues.

Early trials by Flight Refuelling during 1981-1982 into a cost effective target tug to replace the Canberra involved the use of SwedAir Cessna 441s and Mitsubishi Mu-2s. The target towing fitment can just be seen under the fuselage of this Mu-2 – the wingtip pods are fuel tanks.

Parked on their ramp on the north-east side of the airport, these Falcon 20s await their next duty for the Royal Navy. One major operation is the weekly 'Thursday War' exercise involving warships exercising in the English Channel.

Dornier 228s were operated by FR Aviation on Fisheries Patrol duties between 1986 and 1998, since when they have continued their surveillance duties under other contracts. Returning to base, one of the Dorniers flies over the Needles Lighthouse on the Isle of Wight.

The Falcons frequently operate in pairs, and sometimes return to base in threes, but four is unusual. The pilots of these four are practising their formation-keeping skills in preparation for their appearance at the 1994 Farnborough Air Show.

The RAF's remaining fleet of English Electric Canberras were overhauled by FR Aviation during the 1990s. This is a TT.18 target tug version, whilst in the background is the large hangar erected by the company during 1990 for the conversion of RAF VC.10s.

Right: Work underway on one of the VC.10 underwing pylons that would hold the new refuelling pod. As well as the necessary fuel pipe plumbing, anti-corrosion work was also carried out on the aircraft during their overhauls, prior to their return to 10 Squadron at Brize Norton.

Below: FR Aviation's 'VC.10 Hangar' in 1992 with conversion work under way on two RAF VC.10 transports. Conversion involved the fitting of underwing refuelling pods, plus a re-worked cockpit, to make the aircraft dual role tanker/transports.

Following the award of the contact for the rebuilding of RAF Nimrods under British Aerospace's Nimrod 2000 Project, FR Aviation erected a further hangar during 1998. Later work undertaken included the conversion of Boeing 727 airliners into freighters.

The Nimrod 2000 programme required FR Aviation to completely strip down existing Nimrod fuselages prior to the fitting of new wings and engines. To get the initial fuselages to Bournemouth in 1997 they were flown from Kinloss inside an Antonov An-124 freighter.

Six
Additional Businesses & Operations

Over the years there have been various aviation companies at the airport – overhaul businesses, flying clubs and vintage jet operators. These have all helped towards the development of the airport.

The College of Air Traffic Control and its associated Evaluation Unit were originally established at Aldermaston in 1947, moving to Bournemouth the following year to undertake the training of controllers. In the early days the trainee plotters needed to see something on their radar screens, this being provided by a fleet of Consuls and Doves which flew circuits to provide 'blips'. The introduction of computers in 1975 did away with the need for real aircraft. A brand new college was built in 1962, and in 1995 the Evaluation Unit became the Air Traffic Management Development Centre, undertaking research and development on behalf of NATS and the College.

Airwork Services moved its HQ and overhaul business to Bournemouth in 1960. Originally dealing with airliners, the business became military orientated by 1980 with contracts to overhaul FRADU Hunters and aircraft of the Sultan of Oman Air Force. Airwork were acquired by Short Bros. in 1994, running down the overhaul work, but retaining their HQ. Following the departure of British Aerospace, much of their site was taken over by Lovaux in 1984 for the overhaul and repair of military aircraft. This included the FRADU Hunter contract from 1988-91, but by this time the company was part of the FLS Aerospace Group, becoming more airliner orientated. FLS set up a Light Aircraft Division in 1991 with the intention of producing the Edgley Optica and the Trago SAH-1. Production of five of each was undertaken in 1993, following which FLS tried to sell the production lines as a package, but without success. AIM Aviation also took over some of the British Aerospace hangars, their main business being the design and installation of aircraft interiors, plus some respray work. In 1991 they obtained a contract from Saab Aircraft to paint all their new Saab 2000 airlines, which were flown to Bournemouth in 'factory green'. The contract covered 250 aircraft, but sales proved disappointing and Saab finished production in 1999 after only sixty had been produced. Amongst the variety of aircraft seen recently have been a DRA Harrier and Tornado, as well as various Islanders.

The Citation Centre was established by IDS Fanjets in 1979, taking up one of the wartime hangars. IDS soon became an authorized service centre for the Citation range of executive jets, business expanding to cater for this increasing section of the travel market. Acquired by CSE Aviation of Oxford in 1999, the company moved into a new hangar in the summer of 2000. Capable of holding eight of the growing range of Citations, the hangar receives aircraft from all over Europe for attention.

When British Airways retired its fleet of One-Elevens in 1991 they were flown to Bournemouth for storage. In 1993 sixteen were purchased by European Aviation with the intention of overhauling them prior to resale. A change of direction saw the company enter the airline business in its own right, also chartering the One-Elevens to major airlines. The company set up a maintenance division in the same hangars in which BAC had originally built the airliners, also handling One-Elevens of other operators. Early in 1998 European acquired Sabena's fleet of Boeing 737s, and gradually these began to replace the One-Elevens which were forced out of the sky by new regulations due to their noisy Spey engines. The final scheduled service was flown from Bournemouth on 30 December 2001, with farewell flights for enthusiasts on 16 and 31 March 2002. European moved into the long haul business with the purchase of five Boeing 747s from British Airways in December 2001. These were mainly employed for charter activities, operating from Gatwick and Manchester, with only positioning flights being undertaken from Bournemouth. However, flights to the United States from Bournemouth are a possibility.

The Bournemouth Flying Club was formed in the autumn of 1961, perpetuating the name used at Christchurch airfield in the 1930s. From small beginnings in a wartime wooden hut, expansion over the years meant the need to move to larger premises on the north-east side of the airport. Acquired by the Norris family in the summer of 1980, it continued its activities with the usual selection of Cessnas and Pipers as part of A&G Aviation. Anglo American Airmotive was an associated company, which in 1993 became the UK agent for the New Piper range of light aircraft. This continued until February 2002 when the agency and business passed to Meridian Aviation, the Flying Club having also changed hands.

The summer of 1981 saw the arrival of Mike Carlton's scarlet Hunter which appeared on the display circuit as Hunter One. Further classic jet fighters arrived including a Meteor and Vampire, but regrettably Mike was killed in an air crash in August 1986. The aircraft were put up for auction, but luckily most remained at Bournemouth to become the basis of Jet Heritage in February 1989. The company carried on with the theme of preserving and displaying classic British jets, also obtaining the contract to prepare aircraft for the Royal Jordanian Air Force Historic Flight. This involved two Vampires and four Hunters, being delivered to Amman in 1997. Another aim was achieved with the opening of a museum in May 1998, following which there were changes to the company including the end of overhauls. The museum now runs separately under the name of Bournemouth Aviation Museum, and in March 2000 de Havilland Aviation arrived to re-establish overhaul work on the aircraft. They also set up their own Historic Flight consisting of a Vampire, Venom and Sea Vixen – classic de Havilland twin boomers. Historic jet fighters were also housed at Bournemouth by Source Classic Jets, who arrived in May 1993 with four Vampire trainers. Further Vampires and Venoms were acquired, and by the summer of 1997 Source were able to put up an eight ship formation. Air show appearances were made at Fairford and Farnborough, but in 2001 the fleet was put up for sale.

The Airport's main industrial area is on the north-western side, the signboard in 1973 showing the users as BAC (Operating) and Airwork Services. The security hut is a remainder from wartime years when it was used as a flight office.

Plenty of work underway in Airwork Services' hangar 102 in 1960. From left to right are Sudan Airways DC-3 ST-AAH, Marconi's radar trials Viking G-AHOP and Dove G-AJJF. At the present time hangar 102 is occupied by Channel Express' engineering division.

95

The Air Shows held during the 1970 and 1980s were always popular with the public, with the later ones being organized by the IAT team of Fairford fame. Making a low pass during the 1980 Air Pageant is preserved USAAF Douglas B-26 Invader N3710G.

Ever since production of the Britten Norman Islander began at Bembridge in 1967, they have frequently visited Bournemouth on test flights or on delivery to their purchaser. This plain-looking example in 1976 is destined for Jonas Aircraft of New York – the US Distributors.

The Bournemouth Flying Club originally operated from Christchurch airfield in the late 1930s, and was re-formed at Bournemouth in September 1961. Bournair was the Air Taxi division, and this blister style hangar was erected in the early 1970s.

Ah! de Havilland! One of the original Bournemouth Flying Club's fleet at Christchurch was Gipsy Moth G-AAHI. After many years of restoration it called at the airport in September 1996 to visit its owner of sixty years before.

Jet Heritage will always be associated with Hawker Hunters. During the mid-1990s they overhauled four Hunters and two Vampires for the Royal Jordanian Air Force Historic Flight, and here two of the Hunters prepare to depart for Amman in May 1997.

Not quite what it seems. This is not a 4 FTS Hunter T.7, but Jet Heritage's G-BOOM in pseudo military marking for film work during October 1982. *Return to Fairborough* was a TV movie starring Robert Mitchum, but he did not visit the airport during the filming.

To mark the fourtieth anniversary of his obtaining the World Air Speed record in September 1953, Neville Duke was reunited with a Hawker Hunter at Jet Heritage in 1993 so that he could fly the course once more – this time as a passenger in G-BOOM.

European Aviation's hangars housed Hawker Sea Fury N36SF for a few months during 1995-1996. Whilst awaiting air show duties, it was normal practise for the historic fighter to be given a monthly air test by its owner.

Source Classic Jets arrived at the airport in May 1993 with a fleet of de Havilland Vampires and Venoms. Four of the fighters attended the International Air Tattoo at Fairford in July 1997, along with The Heritage Pair from Jet Heritage.

For the 1995 season one of the Source Vampires was painted to represent the prototype Vampire that undertook the first jet carrier deck landings in December 1945. In December it flew in formation with another Vampire, plus two Sea Harriers, over HMS *Illustrious* in the Channel.

As a change to the usual military Lockheed Hercules, the airport was visited a number of times during the early 1980s by the brightly coloured aircraft of Safair. ZS-RSF is being loaded with freight in March 1985 prior to its return to South Africa.

Bournemouth has been visited by freight aircraft collecting equipment from Oil Spill Response Ltd of Southampton before flying to the site of an oil spill, such as the sinking of a tanker. Ilyushin Il-76s were used in the early 1990s, with Hercules in use at the present time.

Pleasure flights were provided from in front of the terminal in the 1970s and 1980s by Captain Johnnie in his de Havilland Fox Moth and Piper Caribbean. This was the sight that greeted him on the morning of 2 September 1983 following gales during the night.

In October 1991 FLS Aerospace acquired the production rights to the Trago Mills SAH-1 basic trainer. Modifications were carried out to the original prototype which appeared as the FLS Sprint in May 1992, with production dependent on sufficient orders being received.

AIM Aviation obtained the contract to paint factory 'green' Saab 2000 on behalf of Saab Aircraft. The contract covered 250 aircraft, with the first arriving at Bournemouth in the summer of 1993. Unfortunately poor sales limited production of the airliner to only sixty.

In the mid-1980s much of the former British Aerospace site was taken over by Lovaux for repair and overhaul work, initially on military aircraft. Here in February 1988 a Short Belfast freighter delivers two former Qatar Air Force Hawker Hunters to their hangar.

In the early 1990s Warbirds of Great Britain housed their fleet of Second World War fighters in a specially built hangar at the airport. They were seen infrequently, but usually emerged once a month to undertake engine runs, as with this P-51D Mustang.

Warbirds of Great Britain acquired their fighters from all around the world – this Supermarine Spitfire XVIII SM969 having been found derelict in India. The Bournemouth hangar was just for storage, maintenance work was undertaken at Biggin Hill.

European Aviation's Air Charter division had a fleet of Airbus A.300s, Boeing 737s and BAC One-Elevens available for charter during the mid-1990s. Further 737s were added in 1998 with the purchase of Sabena's fleet of thirteen.

European Aviation took over One-Eleven maintenance work from Lovaux in 1995, and as well as their own fleet they looked after the aircraft of other operators, including the Royal Air Force of Oman. The hangar is the same one the aircraft were originally built in.

A Virgin A.60 Lightship was used by the Conservative Party for publicity during their Bournemouth Conference in October 1996. 'Opportunity for All' was their slogan of the time. The Lightship was also used by the police to aid their security operations at the Conference.

A number of drilling rigs have visited the Dorset coastline searching for gas and oil, with crews being flown out by helicopter. Here suitably dressed crew members board Bristow Helicopters Bell 212 G-BALZ in October 1993 for the flight to Elf's *Penned* 85 in Poole Bay.

The CSE Citation Centre moved into a new hangar on the north side during the summer of 2000. They are an approved service centre for the expanding range of Citations, their hangar being able to hold eight of the executive jets.

Aircraft within the Bournemouth Aviation Museum range from this Isaacs Fury G-BZAS to a One-Eleven airliner. The majority of the aircraft are maintained in an airworthy condition, including classic Hunter, Meteor and Vampire jet fighters.

Illustrating the point that you never know what might turn up at Bournemouth. Two Kamov Ka-32 helicopters clattered out of the mid-day sky on 15 September 1994 to refuel whilst en route from Dublin to Nantes.

Another Russian visitor. Being one of three which visited FLS Aerospace, Tupolev Tu-134 YL-LBF arrived in bare metal from Riga in January 1994 for a respray. It is seen a few days later awaiting return to LatCharter.

In the summer of 1980 the Flying Club was acquired by A&G Aviation, who expanded facilities over the years. Associated company Anglo American Airmotive became UK agents for Piper Aircraft in 1993. These Cherokees are destined for the Doha Flying College in Qatar.

Anglo American held the UK launch of the Malibu Meridian turboprop executive in June 2001, since when the Piper Agency has passed to Meridian Aviation. Aircraft are flown across the Atlantic to Bournemouth – with additional fuel tanks being a requirement!

Aircraft resprays have been undertaken by a number of firms at the airport. Spitfire XVI TE184 was painted in French AF markings during June 2000 by Airtime Aviation, and is seen inside one of the wartime hangars awaiting collection by its owner.

De Havilland Aviation set up an engineering base next to the Aviation Museum in March 2000, undertaking work on their classic de Havilland twin boom jet fighters. These included the sole remaining airworthy Sea Vixen, which returned to the Air Show circuit in May 2001.

Seven

Present Day Operations

In June 1994 Bournemouth and Dorset Councils, as the airport company shareholders, confirmed they were seeking private sector finance to enable development and expansion of the airport to proceed. Both realized they would be unable to raise sufficient funds from their ratepayers – the proposed runway extension alone would cost £1.6 million. However it was stipulated that any expansion would be within the existing boundary, encompassing 970 acres, and that mid-range airliners such as Boeing 767s were anticipated – not jumbo jets. By the beginning of the following year the plan had changed, with the Councils confirming that they were going ahead with the sale of the airport. In April 1995 the National Express Group purchased a 999 year lease for £7.13 million, the Group already owning East Midlands Airport. In June they confirmed the runway would be extended by 20%, thereby hoping to attract scheduled services, IT operators and freight traffic to serve markets in the south. Constructed during the following winter, the extension was ready the following April – but who could open it? The directors decided not to seek a person, but to bring Concorde in to open the runway on 21 April 1996 – 'Big Nose Day'. The Concorde operated a charter from and to Heathrow organized by Bath Travel. The event attracted huge crowds which demonstrated to the new owners that there was interest in the airport – people just needed to be persuaded to use it. There were no scheduled services at the time, only the Mediterranean holiday IT flights, so Ryanair took the opening as the time to announce a Dublin service as from May, quickly proving to be very popular. May also saw the first transatlantic charter by Bath Travel who filled a UK Leisure Boeing 767 to Orlando, and Thomson Holidays used a 767 for its summertime IT holiday flights to Majorca. A new range of IT flights was introduced by Islanders Holidays from the summer of 1996, initially including the Channel Islands and Gerona. A second scheduled service was added in September 1997 when Euroscot Express commenced services to Edinburgh and Glasgow with a BAC One-Eleven. This was replaced by an ATR.72 in August 1998, at which time it was hoped to add a route to Amsterdam, but unfortunately, like many before, the airline went out of business in July 1999. There were further Concorde charters, including passengers sailing to New York on the QE2 and returning home to Bournemouth by Concorde. Flying time was three hours eight minutes, compared with twenty-four hours in 1945! From the autumn of 1999 Palmair introduced a Boeing 737 on its IT flights, giving greater range and capacity than their BAe.146. The 737 was also used on an increasingly popular range of day trips to various European cities – so keeping the aircraft fully utilized.

After the runway extension, National Express's next proposal was for a larger terminal, with plans being drawn up during 1997. Although approved at local level in 1998, National Express decided to delay building the terminal as passenger numbers had not risen as anticipated. A further blow came the following year when the Government called in the plans for review as part of the land fell within 'Green Belt', so the terminal was 'put on ice'. On the bright side, a number of high profile businesses were moving into newly built accommodation on the Aviation Park West, for example Honeywell and VT Aerospace.

Channel Express has greatly expanded over the years, with express parcels and freight operations throughout Europe and the Middle East with a fleet of Airbus A.300F Eurofreighters and Boeing 737QCs. Fokker F.27s still operate services from Bournemouth to the Channel Islands, also undertaking the nightly Royal Mail flights. The company retains its headquarters at the airport, and also its Parts Trading division which has grown recently, acquiring six A.300s to provide spare parts for airlines throughout Europe and the USA. The majority of IT holiday flights currently offered from Bournemouth are to the Mediterranean, plus winter ski flights to the Alps and fly/cruise holidays to the Caribbean. Early in 2001 Palmair was voted the third best airline in the world by *Holiday Which?*, carrying 50,000 holidaymakers a year. 2002 saw Ryanair introduce a new service from Frankfurt/Hahn in February. The airline had been expanding during a difficult economic climate for airlines, and had introduced a fleet of New Generation Boeing 737s.

In September 2000 the National Express Group announced that the airport, along with East Midlands, was being put up for auction so that they could concentrate on their bus and rail divisions. Other airports were also changing hands at this time – Bristol was sold by First Group and Prestwick was sold by Stagecoach. In March 2001 Manchester Airport completed the purchase of both Bournemouth and East Midlands Airports for £241 million, explaining 'Regional airports have a crucial role and we intend to make Bournemouth more successful. Bournemouth is well placed to capture forecast growth in the south'. The new £1.25 million terminal had not been forgotten by National Express, who had submitted revised plans during 2000 with a new siting. Environmental issues were addressed, as the airport needed to retain its good neighbour policy with the local community. Planning permission was received in September 2001, and Manchester Airport confirmed that it would proceed with its construction when the economic time was right.

Over the years the airport has seen many ups and downs. Following the worldwide downturn in air travel in the autumn of 2001, Bournemouth International Airport is well placed to cater for the upturn in business that will soon return.

Bournemouth International Airport viewed from the north in 1998, showing the extension of the main runway to the right. The terminal area is situated middle left, FR Aviation bottom left and European Aviation (former BAC factory) bottom right.

A 1996 view of the North West Industrial area, the majority of which was the former British Aircraft Corporation One-Eleven production site. One-Elevens of European Aviation are seen parked outside the hangars.

The present terminal, built for Channel Islands' traffic, has sufficient check-in and refreshment areas, but lacks space in its arrival and departure areas. To cope with additional passengers on holiday flights, plans have been passed for the building of a replacement terminal.

Over the years, the majority of the wartime buildings in the terminal area have been demolished, sometimes to be replaced by modern ones. Others have gone to make additional space for expanding the aircraft parking apron area.

The Airport's Fire Crew stand proudly in front of their new Boughton Barracuda fire tender received in September 1998. Capable of crossing all types of terrain quickly, its main purpose is to cover a burning aircraft with foam at a very high rate.

Safety considerations mean the Fire Crew can no longer practise their drill on an old aircraft. This purpose built rig was installed during 2000 to simulate various types of aircraft. The 'fuselage' represents a Boeing 737 and 747 and the 'wing' a propeller or jet engine.

Always the best view of an airport. Controllers in Bournemouth's Tower are responsible for control of aircraft within the airport's zone, and, as can be seen, they have a clear view overlooking the main runway.

Externally little can be seen of the Control Tower's wartime origins, but the basic building is still contained in the middle of all the later extensions. Preparing for a run and break are the BAe Hawks of the Red Arrows.

During the late 1990s Bournemouth was visited by a number of Lockheed Tristars – some for 'cheap' parking and others for scrapping. Air Atlanta of Iceland's TF-ABU used the airport for parking in December 1997 as it was cheaper than staying at Gatwick.

One does not normally associate Virgin with Bournemouth, but this Boeing 737 of Virgin Express was a last minute replacement on a holiday flight to Alicante for another Boeing which had gone unserviceable earlier in the day.

Concorde first landed at the airport on the aptly named 'Big Nose Day' in order to open the extension to the main runway. Crowds flocked to the airport and surrounding roads to view the supersonic airliner, which has since operated a number of other charters.

Following the opening of the runway extension in May 1996, the first of a number of transatlantic holiday flights was flown by UK Leisure Boeing 767 G-UKLI to Orlando, Florida. This is the type of holiday flight that the airport intends to develop over the years.

As a replacement for the well-liked Lockheed Electra freighter, Channel Express acquired their first Boeing 737 in the summer of 2001. Their 'Quick Change' variant has a large freight door, but is also capable of carrying a full passenger load.

European Aviation's Air Charter division used their fleet of One-Elevens for sub-charter holiday flights for many major airlines. They remained in service until March 2002 when new regulations grounded them in Europe due to their noisy Spey engines.

Open wide! The Airbus Beluga visited in January 2000 to collect a large section of an Airbus A.300 airliner fuselage. This was from an aircraft dismantled by Channel Express for spares, with the fuselage being sold back to Airbus for use as a ground demonstrator.

Dakota operations at Bournemouth spanned sixty years, having started with USAAF C-47s in November 1942. The final operator was South Coast Airways which offered nostalgic flights in this luxury-equipped version until ceasing operations in July 2002.

A guaranteed crowd-puller is the visit of the Red Arrows for their annual seafront display over Bournemouth Pier. The Hawks also use the airport to refuel when undertaking other local displays, and the 2001 team pose in front of one of their scarlet mounts.

The big one! The largest aircraft to use the airport is the Antonov An-124 freighter. This Russian aircraft has to be used for outsize loads as the West has nothing else available. Here the ground crew await the lowering of the aircraft's front ramp so that they can start unloading.

Not all Ryanair flights are provided with a group of Irish dancers. The special occasion here was the inaugural flight from Bournemouth to Dublin in May 1996. For such events Ryanair operate their Boeing 737 EI-CKS which is painted with large titles to maximize publicity.

Ryanair are happy to use their aircraft as flying advertising hordings. This one publicises the *News of the World* on one side and *The Sun* on the opposite. Other Boeings in their fleet have publicised Hertz Rentals, Jaguar Cars, Kilkenny Beer, as well as one-offs for Red Nose Day.

To avoid the problems of finding suitable carriers for their holiday flights, Bath Travel's Palmair Division set up its own airline, commencing services in May 1993 with BAe 146 G-BPNT. From November 1999 it was replaced by a Boeing 737 – offering greater capacity and range.

Holidaymakers boarding Palmair European's Boeing 737 for their flight to the sun. Palmair was voted the third best airline in the world by *Holiday Which?* magazine in the spring of 2001 – how many other airlines have their chairman come to say farewell to every flight?

Bournemouth saw its first Jumbo Jet in May 2000. Seen landing is a 747SP VIP version which currently uses the airport for cheap parking in between flights from London to the Middle East. Lightly loaded, there is little noise on takeoff to attract the local residents.

European Aviation took a big step forward in December 2001 when they purchased five former British Airways Boeing 747s. Only positioning flights are undertaken from their home base, with charter services being operated from larger airports.

The old British Airways colour scheme, seen on BAe ATP G-MANF of British Regional Airways which, on this occasion in 2002, had been diverted from Southampton. As well as other diversions, British Airways ATPs were also used on Jersey holiday flights during 1996.

One of British Airways' 'exotic' tail colour schemes is seen on a BAe RJ 100, the type used to operate weekly winter ski flights to Chambery on behalf of Crystal Holidays. By 2002 they had returned to the more tasteful Union Flag colour scheme.

The pilot of Britannia Airways Boeing 767 G-BRIG awaits his passengers at the start of the first stage of their holiday to the Caribbean, where they will enjoy a fourteen day cruise around the islands, and hopefully plenty of sunshine.

Currently winter ski flights are operated to Chambery, Innsbruck and Turin. Inghams use Tyrolean Airways for the weekly service to Innsbruck, and returning passengers leave this Canadair Regional Jet. Tyrolean have also used Dash Eights and Fokker 70s for the flights.

Recent years have seen more diversions from Southampton due either to poor visibility or strong crosswinds. One of a number of aircraft on 15 January 1997 was Air France ATR.42 F-GGLR seen arriving from Paris CDG.

Ryanair commenced its service to Frankfurt Hann on 14 February 2002 – Valentine's Day. To mark the occasion the boarding passengers were greeted with hearts and cupids on the side of Boeing 737 EI-CSF.

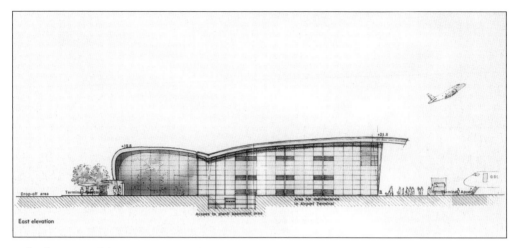

Side elevation of the airport's new futuristic terminal building, for which plans have now been passed after a long delay. The terminal presently awaits the upturn in aviation business in order to receive the final go-ahead.

Michael Green, Chairman of the Airport's Management Committee in 1969 and now Chairman of the Southern Tourist Board, hands over the 2001 Welcome Host award to Managing Director Glyn Jones. Members of the airport's 'Welcoming' staff look on.